Maths
made easy

Key Stage 1
ages 6-7
Beginner

Author Sue Phillips
Consultant Sean McArdle

Certificate

Congratulations to .... *charlie* ....
(write your name here)
for successfully finishing this book.

☆ *You're a star!* ☆

DK

Numbers

Which numbers are the snakes hiding?

1	2	3	4	5		7	8	9	
11	12	13		15			18	19	
21	22	23	24		26	27	28		
31				35	36		38	39	40
41				45		47	48	49	50
	52	53	54	55		57	58	59	60
61		63	64	65				69	70
		73	74		76	77	78	79	80
81	82		84					88	
		93		95	96			98	

| 6 | |
| 16 | 17 |

| 10 |
| 20 |
| 29 | 30 |

| 32 | 33 | 34 |
| | | |

| 14 |
| 25 |

| 30 |
| 25 |

| 15 |
| 26 |

Read, write, and draw

Write the numbers and draw the pictures.

76	seventy-six	

59		

	forty-five	

112	one hundred and twelve	

107		

	one hundred and fifty	

3

Counting

Count forwards or backwards in 10s.
Write the missing numbers.

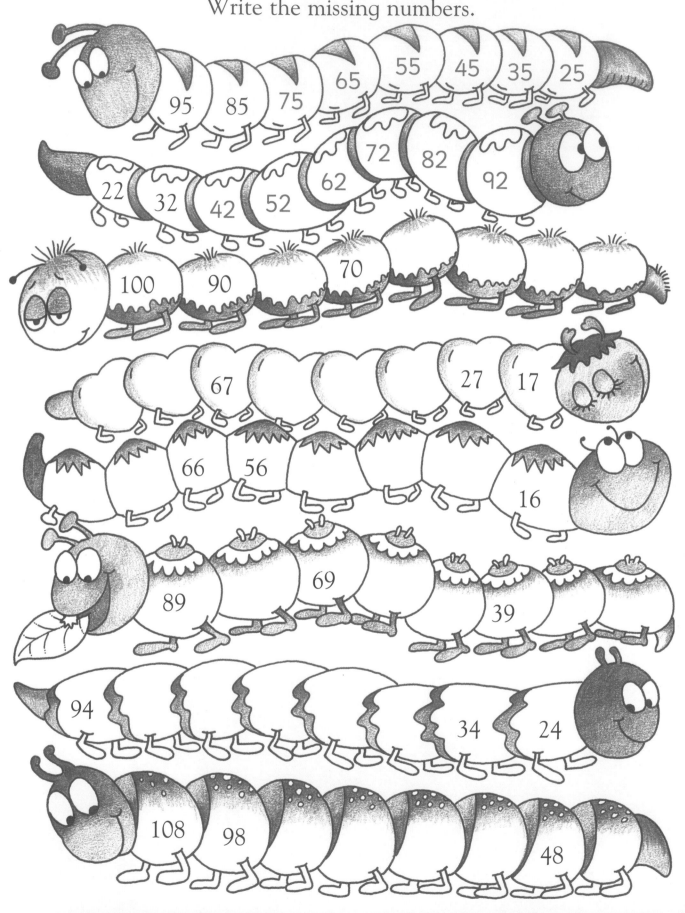

95 85 75 65 55 45 35 25

22 32 42 52 62 72 82 92

100 90 70

67 27 17

66 56 16

89 69 39

94 34 24

108 98 48

Odd or even?

Add or take away to find the answers to the sums.
Choose two colours. Colour the odd houses one colour
and the even houses another colour.

32
+4
36

even

23
−4
19

odd

10
−5

11
+2

25
−6

20
+7

23
−7

35
−5

30
−6

16
+8

25
−10

28
−8

17
+9

36
−10

Counting in 3s, 4s, and 5s

Draw, count, and write.

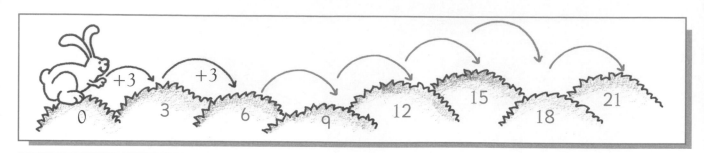

0 +3 3 +3 6 9 12 15 18 21

40 −3 37 −3

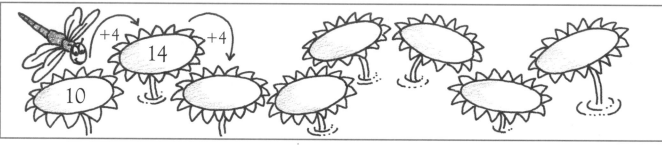

10 +4 14 +4

32 −4 28 −4

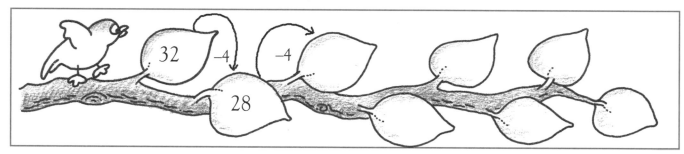

17 +5 22 +5

51 −5 46 −5

2s, 5s, and 10s

Use your 2x, 5x, and 10x tables to help you join the dots.

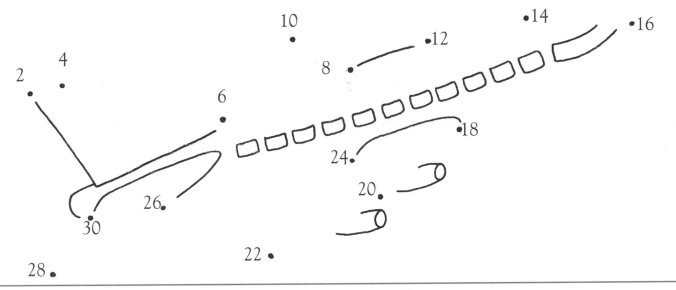

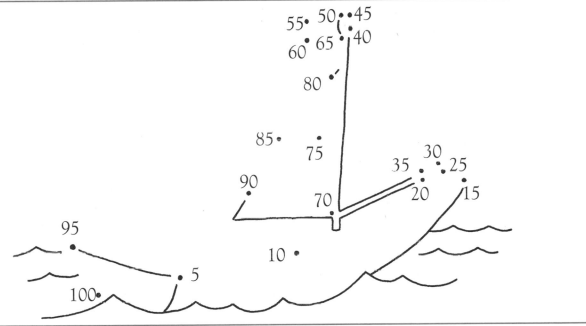

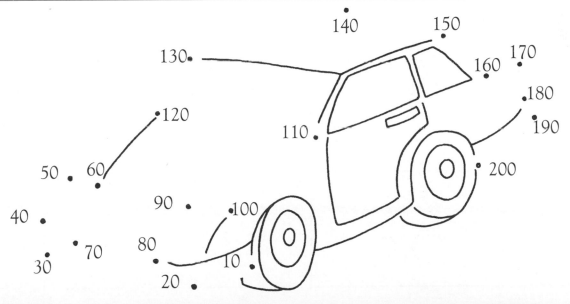

Comparing

Complete the boxes.

2 less		2 more
51	53	55

	In-between		
96	97	98	99

	In-between	
20		24

3 less		3 more
	30	

2 less		2 more
	29	

	In-between	
18		22

	In-between	
131		134

10 less		10 more
	119	

5 less		5 more
	85	

	In-between	
40		45

	In-between	
99		102

5 less		5 more
	156	

Ordering

Write the numbers in order.

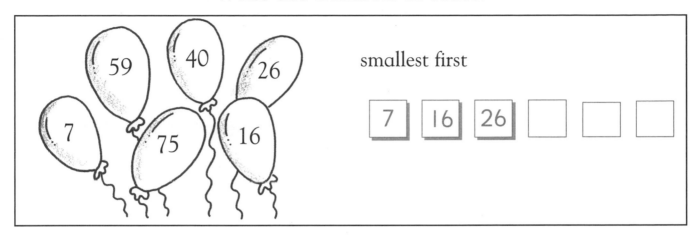

smallest first

| 7 | 16 | 26 | | | |

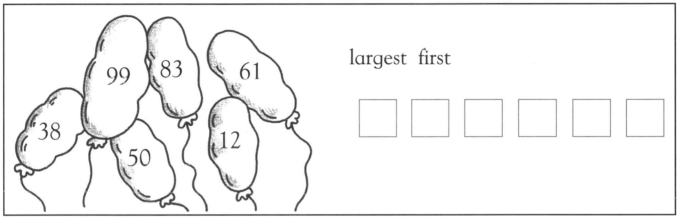

largest first

| | | | | | |

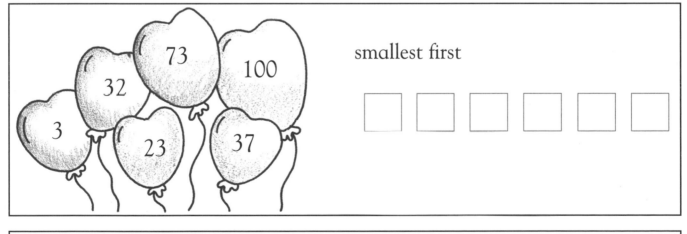

smallest first

| | | | | | |

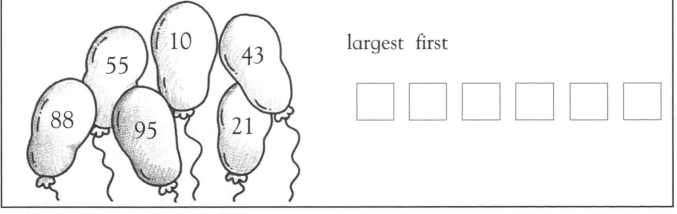

largest first

| | | | | | |

Adding coins

Use three coins each time.
How many different totals can you make?

(5p) + (20p) + (50p) = 75p

(2p) + (1p) + (10p) = 13p

Fractions of shapes

Colour one-third ($\frac{1}{3}$).

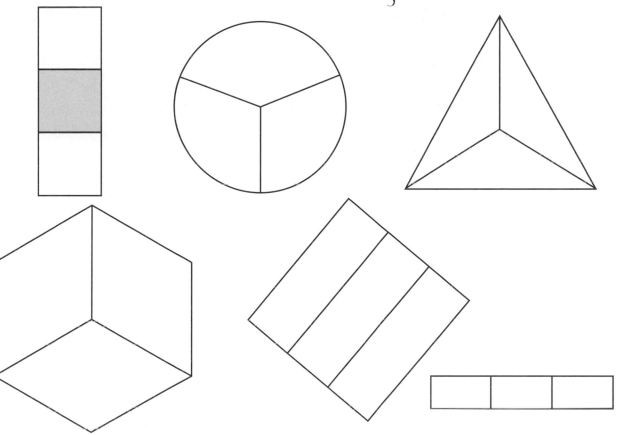

Is it $\frac{1}{3}$? ✓ or ✗.

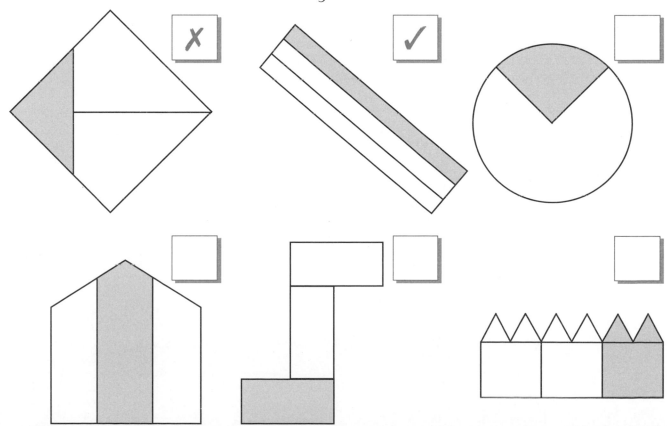

Fractions

Colour one-third ($\frac{1}{3}$) and write how many.

$\frac{1}{3}$ of 9 is $\boxed{3}$

$\frac{1}{3}$ of 12 is ☐

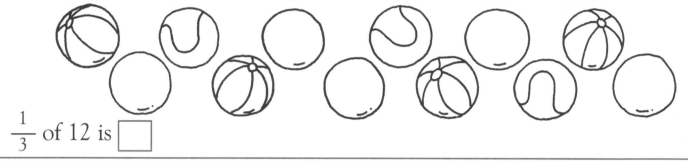

$\frac{1}{3}$ of 6 is ☐

$\frac{1}{3}$ of 3 is ☐

$\frac{1}{3}$ of 15 is ☐

$\frac{1}{3}$ of 18 is ☐

Matching fractions

Colour all the matching squares.

Use yellow for halves.
Use orange for thirds.
Use green for quarters.

$\dfrac{1}{2}$	(dots)	(circle)	(bars)
(triangle)	one-third	one-half	(squares)
(dots)	$\dfrac{1}{4}$	(circle)	one-quarter
$\dfrac{1}{3}$	(dots)	(shape)	(circle)

Label each part.

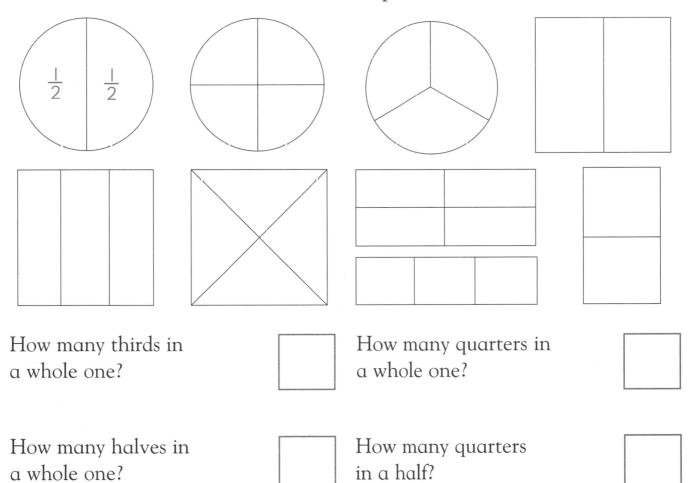

$\frac{1}{2}$	$\frac{1}{2}$	

How many thirds in
a whole one?

How many quarters in
a whole one?

How many halves in
a whole one?

How many quarters
in a half?

13

Number wall

Write all the odd numbers. ☐ ☐ ☐

Add them up and write the total. ☐

Write all the even numbers. ☐ ☐ ☐

Add them up and write the total. ☐

Find three numbers which add up to make 13. ☐ ☐ ☐

Write the smallest number. ☐   Double it. ☐

Write the largest number. ☐   Find $\frac{1}{2}$ of it. ☐

Find two ways of making 10. ☐ + ☐ = 10   ☐ + ☐ = 10

Add up all the numbers on the wall. ☐ + ☐ + ☐ + ☐ + ☐ + ☐ = ☐

Multiplying by 2

How many legs?

 lot of 2 legs ⟶ legs

 x 2 = 2

[ ] lots of 2 legs ⟶ [ ] legs

[ ] x 2 = [ ]

[ ] lots of 2 legs ⟶ [ ] legs

[ ] x 2 = [ ]

[ ] lots of 2 legs ⟶ [ ] legs

[ ] x 2 = [ ]

[ ] lots of 2 legs ⟶ [ ] legs

[ ] x 2 = [ ]

---

2 x table

1 x 2 = [ ]	3 x 2 = [ ]	5 x 2 = [ ]	7 x 2 = [ ]	9 x 2 = [ ]
2 x 2 = [ ]	4 x 2 = [ ]	6 x 2 = [ ]	8 x 2 = [ ]	10 x 2 = [ ]

Multiplying by 10

Count, write the numbers, and say aloud.

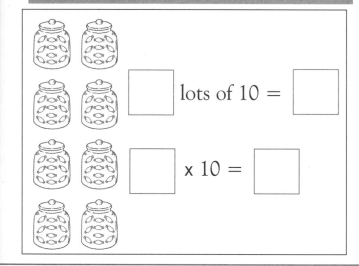

| 2 | lots of 10 = | 20 |

| 2 | x 10 = | 20 |

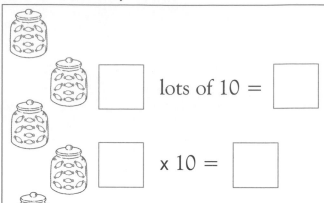

lots of 10 =

x 10 =

lots of 10 =

x 10 =

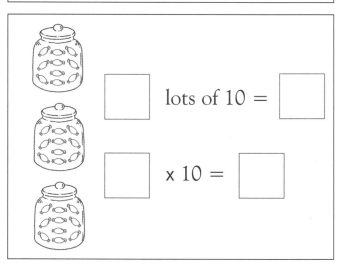

lots of 10 =

x 10 =

Write the answers.

1 x 10 = 　　2 x 10 = 　　3 x 10 = 　　4 x 10 =

5 x 10 = 　　6 x 10 = 　　7 x 10 = 　　8 x 10 =

9 x 10 = 　　10 x 10 =

Write how many lots of 10.

　x 10 = 30　　　　x 10 = 60　　　　x 10 = 40

　x 10 = 90　　　　x 10 = 10　　　　x 10 = 100

Multiplying by 5

How many?

4 lots of 5 = 20

4 x 5 = 20

___ lots of 5 = ___

___ x 5 = ___

___ lots of 5 = ___

___ x 5 = ___

___ lots of 5 = ___

___ x 5 = ___

___ lots of 5 = ___

___ x 5 = ___

___ lots of 5 = ___

___ x 5 = ___

Write the answers.

6 x 5 = 30   9 x 5 = ___   3 x 5 = ___   5 x 5 = ___

10 x 5 = ___   7 x 5 = ___   8 x 5 = ___   6 x 5 = ___

Write how many lots.

40 = 8 x 5   35 = ___ x 5   10 = ___ x 5

20 = ___ x 5   45 = ___ x 5   5 = ___ x 5

Money

You have only 3 coins in each purse. Draw the
3 coins which make the exact amount needed.
You may use each coin more than once.

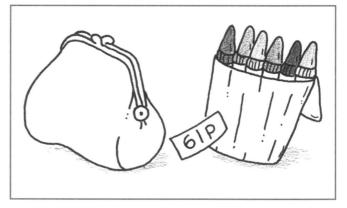

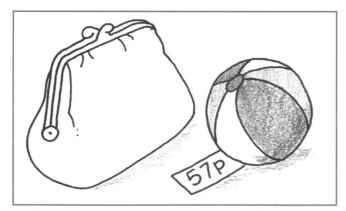

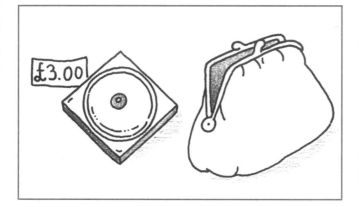

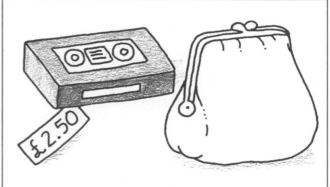

Adding money

Add up the money. Write the totals in the right squares.

+	2p	5p	8p	6p
3p				9p
11p				
29p		34p		
32p				

+	2p	14p	26p	9p	43p
17p					
20p				29p	
33p	35p				
41p					

Using doubles

Use the doubles to answer these sums.

6 + 6 = 12	10 + 10 = 20
6 + 7 6 + 6 + 1 = 13	10 + 11 10 + 10 + 1 = 21
6 + 5 6 + 6 – 1 = 11	10 + 9 10 + 10 – 1 = 19

Use doubles to answer these sums.

4 + 4 = ☐

4 + 5 = ☐ + ☐ + 1 = ☐

4 + 3 = ☐ + ☐ – 1 = ☐

7 + 7 = ☐

7 + 8 = ☐ + ☐ + 1 = ☐

7 + 6 = ☐ + ☐ – 1 = ☐

8 + 8 = ☐

9 + 9 = ☐ + ☐ + 1 = ☐

7 + 7 = ☐ + ☐ – 1 = ☐

Double your doubles.

2	double it	4	double it	8	9	double it	☐	double it	☐
10	double it	☐	double it	☐	11	double it	☐	double it	☐
14	double it	☐	double it	☐	7	double it	☐	double it	☐

Adding up

Add up the numbers on the sails. Write the totals on the boats.

Add the numbers. Write the totals.

$3 + 4 + 12 =$ | 19 | $9 + 9 + 50 =$ | | $7 + 70 + 3 =$ | |

$5 + 49 + 2 =$ | | $23 + 7 + 9 =$ | | $4 + 5 + 60 =$ | |

$37 + 4 + 3 =$ | | $5 + 59 + 7 =$ | | $84 + 8 + 8 =$ | |

```
   39          18          57          66
 +  8        +  6        +  7        +  5
 +  7        +  5        +  4        +  0
 _____      _____      _____      _____
```

Subtraction tables

Finish each table.

−	2	3	5	10
11	9	8		
15	13			
20				

−	1	6	8	9
14				
19	18	13	11	
25				

−	20	14	27	31
52			25	
48			21	
70				

Counting down

The rocket can only lift off at zero.
Use take aways to get back to 0 in 4 moves.

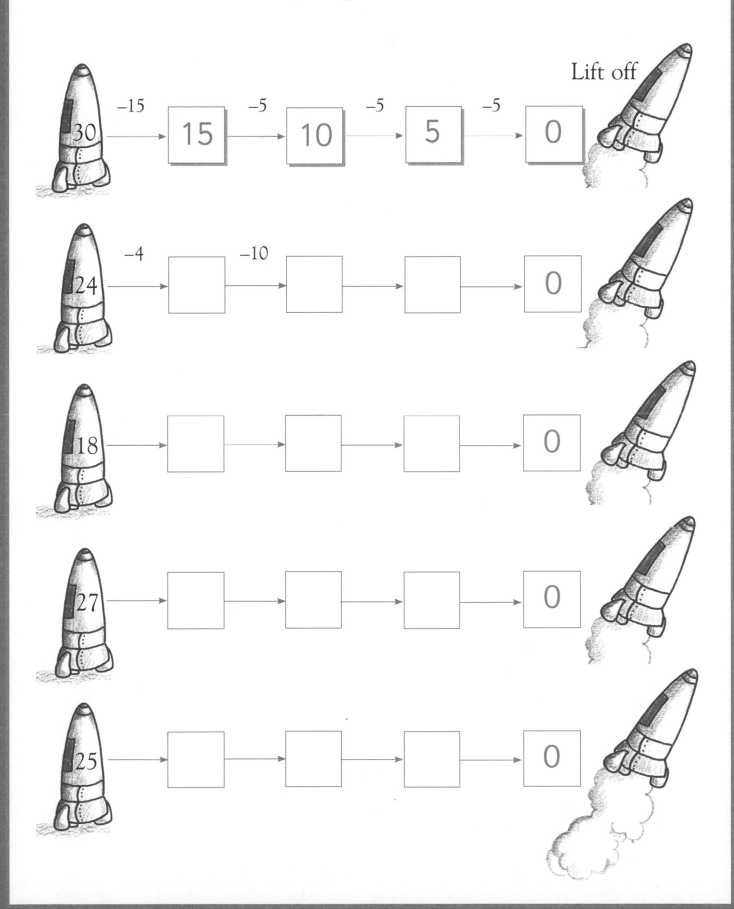

Lift off

30 → −15 → 15 → −5 → 10 → −5 → 5 → −5 → 0

24 → −4 → ☐ → −10 → ☐ → ☐ → 0

18 → ☐ → ☐ → ☐ → 0

27 → ☐ → ☐ → ☐ → 0

25 → ☐ → ☐ → ☐ → 0

Clocks

Write the times under the clocks.

4 o'clock

_____

_____

_____

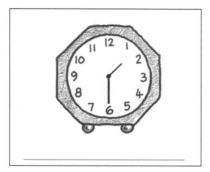

_____

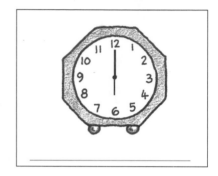

_____

Draw the hands.

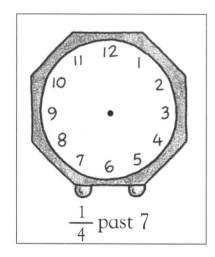

$\frac{1}{4}$ past 7

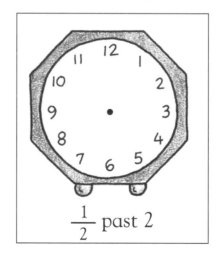

$\frac{1}{2}$ past 2

10 o'clock

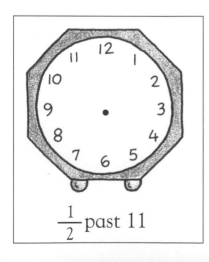

$\frac{1}{2}$ past 11

3 o'clock

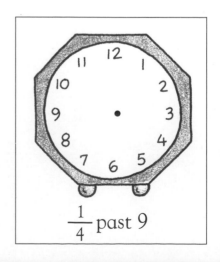

$\frac{1}{4}$ past 9

Clocks and watches

Write the times.

$\frac{1}{4}$ past 4

$\frac{1}{2}$ past 10

5:15

2:45

11:15

10:45

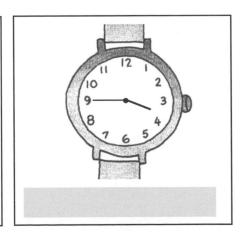

Match the times

Draw a line to link the matching times.

| quarter past nine |

6:15

$\frac{1}{4}$ past 9

| quarter past six |

6:00

| 6 o'clock |

| six o'clock |

9:15

$\frac{1}{4}$ past 6

| half past six |

12:30

| 9 o'clock |

| half past twelve |

9:00

$\frac{1}{2}$ past 6

| nine o'clock |

6:30

$\frac{1}{2}$ past 12

More time

Look at the clocks and write the new times.

one hour later

$\frac{1}{2}$ past 4

one hour earlier

one hour earlier

one hour earlier

one hour later

one hour later

Draw the hands on the clocks to show when the programmes are on.

News	10.00
Animal Safari	10.15
Sports Check	10.45
Joe Giant's Adventures	11.00
Cartoons	11.30

News

Sports Check

Animal Safari

Cartoons

Joe Giant's Adventures

Do you know?

Put the months in order by writing a number on each page.

September
April
February
August
May
March
December
June
November
January 1st
October
July 7th

How many...

... seconds in a minute?

... minutes in an hour?

... hours in a day?

... days in a week?

... days in a year?

... months in a year?

Learn this rhyme.

30 days have September,
April, June, and November.
All the rest have 31,
Except February alone
That has 28 days clear
29 in each leap year.

How many days are there in your birthday month?

Venn diagrams

Flowers with red petals   **Flowers with white petals**

How many flowers ...

... with red petals? **7**   ... with white petals? **10**   ... with both red <u>and</u> white petals? **2**

Shapes with straight sides   **Shapes with curved sides**

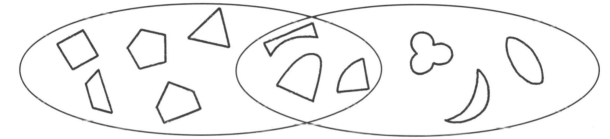

How many shapes ...

... with straight sides? ☐   ... with curved sides? ☐   ... with straight <u>and</u> curved sides? ☐

Odd numbers   **Numbers more than ten**

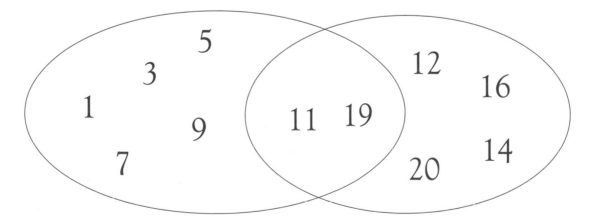

How many numbers are ...

... odd? ☐   ... more than ten? ☐   ... odd <u>and</u> more than ten? ☐

Carroll diagrams

	legs	no legs
green		
not green		

How many creatures are...

... green with no legs	2
... not green	7
... not green with legs	3
... not green with no legs	4

	Shapes that have 4 sides	Shapes that do <u>not</u> have 4 sides
white		
green		

How many shapes are...

... white	
... green with 4 sides	
...white but do <u>not</u> have 4 sides	
... green but do <u>not</u> have 4 sides	

	less than 6	more than 6
odd	1 3 5	7 9 11
even	2 4	8 10 12

How many numbers are...

... odd	
... odd and more than 6	
... even and more than 6	
... less than 6	

2D shapes

Write the name of the shape. Count the corners and sides.

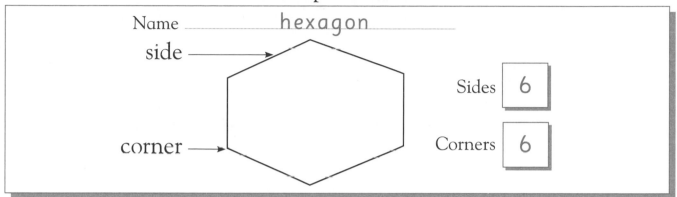

Name ___hexagon___

side ⟶

corner ⟶

Sides | 6

Corners | 6

Name _____

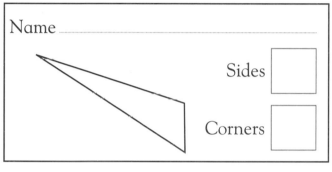

Sides | ☐

Corners | ☐

Name _____

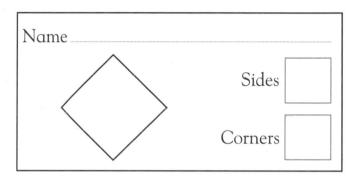

Sides | ☐

Corners | ☐

Name _____

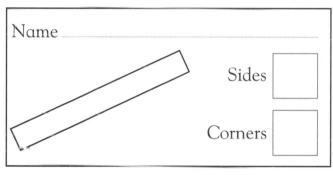

Sides | ☐

Corners | ☐

Name _____

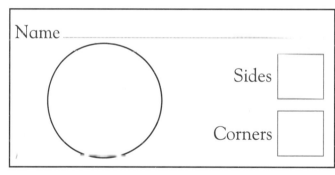

Sides | ☐

Corners | ☐

Name _____

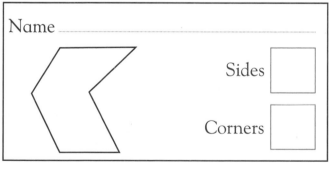

Sides | ☐

Corners | ☐

Name _____

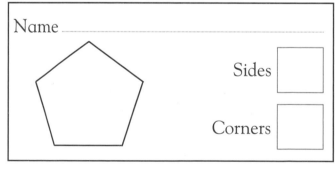

Sides | ☐

Corners | ☐

Name _____

Sides | ☐

Corners | ☐

Name _____

Sides | ☐

Corners | ☐

3D Shapes

Label the 3D shapes.
(cone, cylinder, pyramid, cube, sphere, cuboid)

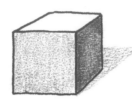  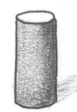

cube
_____   _____   _____   _____

_____   _____

How many of each 3D shape?

cube [3]   cuboid [ ]   cone [ ]   cylinder [ ]

pyramid [ ]   sphere [ ]

Answer Section with Parents' Notes
Key Stage 1
Ages 6–7
Beginner

This 8-page section provides answers to all the activities in this book. This will enable you to mark your children's work or can be used by them if they prefer to do their own marking.

The notes for each page help explain the common pitfalls and problems and, where appropriate, give indications as to what practice is needed to ensure your children understand where they have gone wrong.

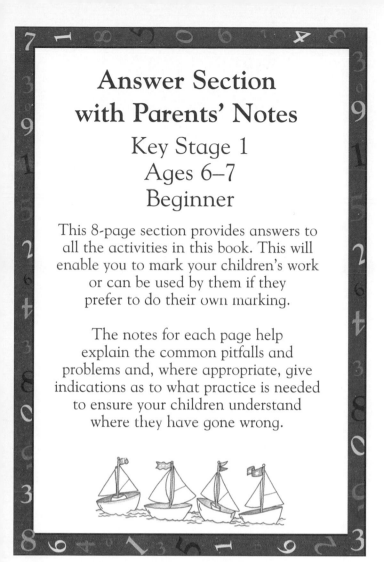

Numbers

Which numbers are the snakes hiding?

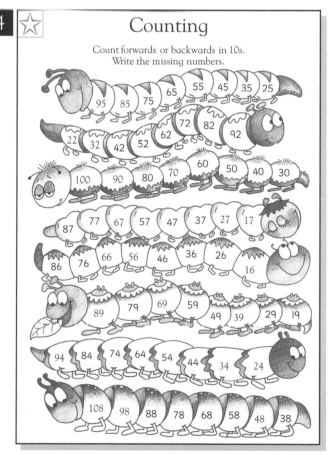

Ask the children how they can be sure that the numbers they have written in the boxes are the ones that have been hidden. Are they relying on only one strategy or are they looking at the columns as well as the rows?

Read, write, and draw

Write the numbers and draw the pictures.

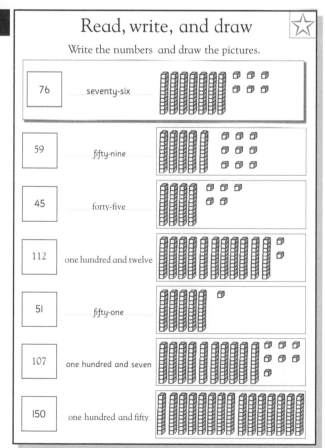

76	seventy-six
59	fifty-nine
45	forty-five
112	one hundred and twelve
51	fifty-one
107	one hundred and seven
150	one hundred and fifty

Do children remember the differing values of each digit? For example, in 170, the '1' is 100, the '7' is 70 and the '0' means no units. In 107, the '0' means no tens and the '7' is only 7 units.

Counting

Count forwards or backwards in 10s.
Write the missing numbers.

Children need to identify whether the numbers are getting smaller or larger, and whether that means they need to count on, or count backwards, by ten. Check that they realise the units digit always stays the same, while the tens digit goes up or down one each time.

Odd or even?

Add or take away to find the answers to the sums.
Choose two colours. Colour the odd houses one colour
and the even houses another colour.

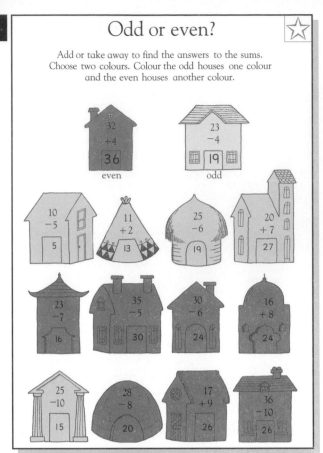

32
+4
36
even

23
−4
19
odd

10
−5
5

11
+2
13

25
−6
19

20
+7
27

23
−7
16

35
−5
30

30
−6
24

16
+8
24

25
−10
15

28
−8
20

17
+9
26

36
−10
26

Can children recite the even and odd sequences (2, 4, 6, 8, 10 and 1, 3, 5, 7, 9)? If they cannot spot a pattern in their answers, show them that starting with two even or two odd numbers always gives an even answer, regardless of whether they are adding or subtracting.

Counting in 3s, 4s, and 5s

Draw, count, and write.

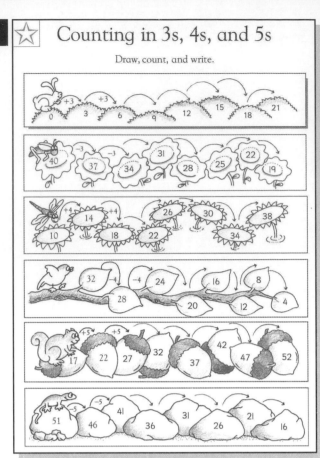

0 +3 3 +3 6 12 15 18 21

40 −3 37 34 31 28 25 22 19

10 +4 14 +4 18 22 26 30 34 38

32 −4 28 −4 24 20 16 12 8 4

17 +5 22 +5 27 32 37 42 47 52

51 −5 46 −5 41 36 31 26 21 16

Remind children to check whether they should be adding or taking away. Subtracting or adding 5 creates a pattern, as the units in the answers go 7, 2, 7, 2 and 1, 6, 1, 6. Can they spot this and predict what the next numbers would be?

2s, 5s, and 10s

Use your 2x, 5x and 10x tables to help you join the dots.

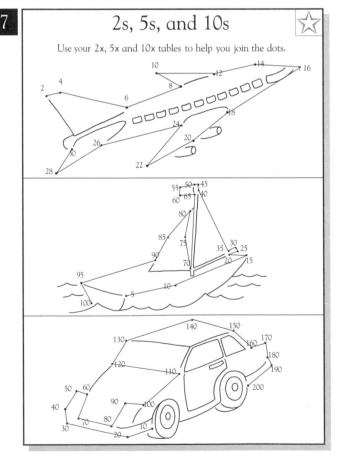

Check whether children can talk about the patterns in the number sequences. Can they recite the 2, 5, or 10 times tables, up to 10 times the number, before they start to join the dots?

Comparing

Complete the boxes.

2 less	In-between		2 more
51	53		55

1 less	In-between		1 more
96	97	98	99

1 less	In-between			1 more
20	21	22	23	24

3 less	In-between	3 more
27	30	33

2 less	In-between	2 more
27	29	31

1 less	In-between			1 more
18	19	20	21	22

1 less	In-between		1 more
131	132	133	134

10 less	In-between	10 more
109	119	129

5 less	In-between	5 more
80	85	90

1 less	In-between	1 more
40	41, 42, 43, 44	45

1 less	In-between		1 more
99	100	101	102

5 less	In-between	5 more
151	156	161

Check whether children can explain the meaning of more, less, and in-between. Can they give examples pertaining to smaller numbers (such as three more or less than 10)? The 'in-between' numbers have been varied so that answers do not follow the same format.

Ordering

Write the numbers in order.

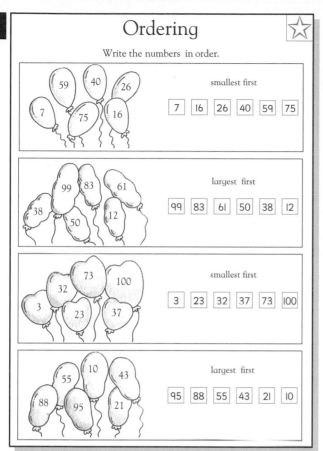

smallest first

| 7 | 16 | 26 | 40 | 59 | 75 |

largest first

| 99 | 83 | 61 | 50 | 38 | 12 |

smallest first

| 3 | 23 | 32 | 37 | 73 | 100 |

largest first

| 95 | 88 | 55 | 43 | 21 | 10 |

Beware of possible reversals such as reading 16 as 61. This indicates a need for more work on place values. In the 3rd section, 23, 32, 37, and 73 have been included to highlight this. Can the children explain the different 'values' of the threes in 37 and 73?

Adding coins

Use three coins each time.
How many different totals can you make?

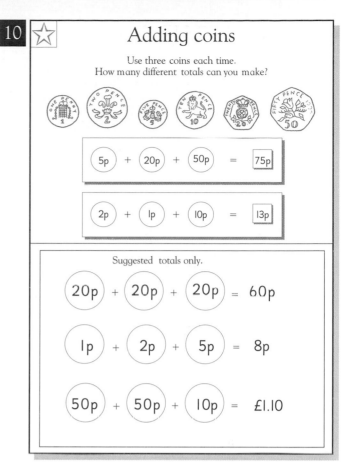

$5p + 20p + 50p = 75p$

$2p + 1p + 10p = 13p$

Suggested totals only.

$20p + 20p + 20p = 60p$

$1p + 2p + 5p = 8p$

$50p + 50p + 10p = £1.10$

If children find adding 50p and 20p coins difficult, cover them up, and do the same activity with only lower value coins. Do they prefer to add up tens first and then count the units? Discuss their methods and let them use their preferred way.

Fractions of shapes

Colour one-third ($\frac{1}{3}$).

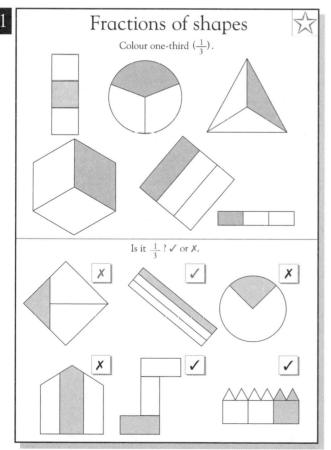

Is it $\frac{1}{3}$? ✓ or ✗.

Explain why some of the pictures in the second section do not have 'one-third' coloured in, even though each shape is cut into three pieces. (The pieces are not all of equal size.) As an extra activity, can the children name any of the shapes they see on the page?

Fractions

Colour one-third ($\frac{1}{3}$) and write how many.

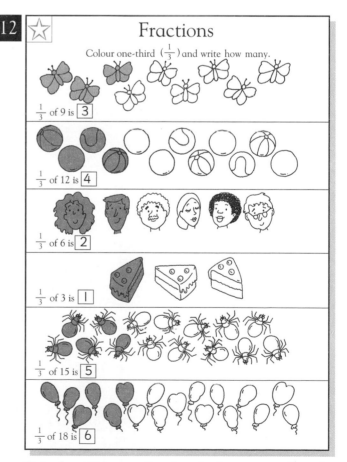

$\frac{1}{3}$ of 9 is 3

$\frac{1}{3}$ of 12 is 4

$\frac{1}{3}$ of 6 is 2

$\frac{1}{3}$ of 3 is 1

$\frac{1}{3}$ of 15 is 5

$\frac{1}{3}$ of 18 is 6

Help the children realise that the bottom number of the fraction indicates how many sets or groups they have to split the objects into.

Matching fractions

Colour the matching squares.

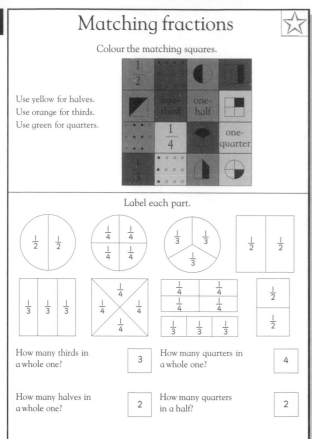

Use yellow for halves.
Use orange for thirds.
Use green for quarters.

Label each part.

How many thirds in a whole one? **3**

How many quarters in a whole one? **4**

How many halves in a whole one? **2**

How many quarters in a half? **2**

If children answer the questions in the final section confidently, a suitable extension would be to ask such questions as, 'How many thirds are there in 3 whole ones?' 'If you had 12 quarters, how many whole ones would it make?'

Number wall

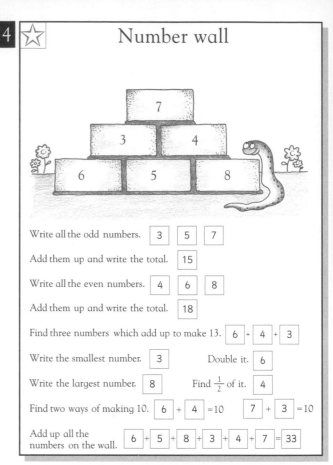

Write all the odd numbers. **3 5 7**

Add them up and write the total. **15**

Write all the even numbers. **4 6 8**

Add them up and write the total. **18**

Find three numbers which add up to make 13. **6** + **4** + **3**

Write the smallest number. **3**   Double it. **6**

Write the largest number. **8**   Find $\frac{1}{2}$ of it. **4**

Find two ways of making 10. **6** + **4** =10   **7** + **3** =10

Add up all the numbers on the wall. **6** + **5** + **8** + **3** + **4** + **7** = **33**

Children may need help reading the questions. Make them look for 'easy options': when adding the even numbers they may recognise that 4 and 6 make 10, to which 8 can then be added . Can they recognise other such addition pairs, without counting on?

Multiplying by 2

How many legs?

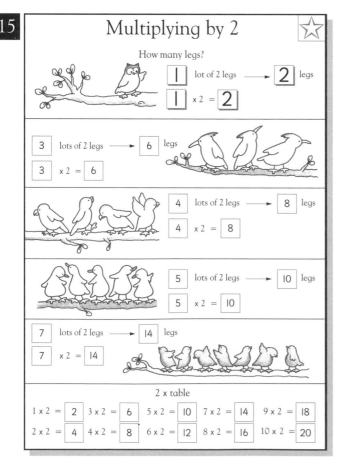

1 lot of 2 legs ⟶ **2** legs
1 x 2 = **2**

3 lots of 2 legs ⟶ **6** legs
3 x 2 = **6**

4 lots of 2 legs ⟶ **8** legs
4 x 2 = **8**

5 lots of 2 legs ⟶ **10** legs
5 x 2 = **10**

7 lots of 2 legs ⟶ **14** legs
7 x 2 = **14**

2 x table

1 x 2 = **2**	3 x 2 = **6**	5 x 2 = **10**	7 x 2 = **14**	9 x 2 = **18**
2 x 2 = **4**	4 x 2 = **8**	6 x 2 = **12**	8 x 2 = **16**	10 x 2 = **20**

Can children see the pattern created by the units digits? They follow 2, 4, 6, 8, 0. Do they know whether these are odd or even numbers? Reciting 2, 4, 6, 8, 10 is easy but can they give you a fast response if you ask them questions like, 'What are 3 lots of 2'?

Multiplying by 10

Count, write the numbers, and say aloud.

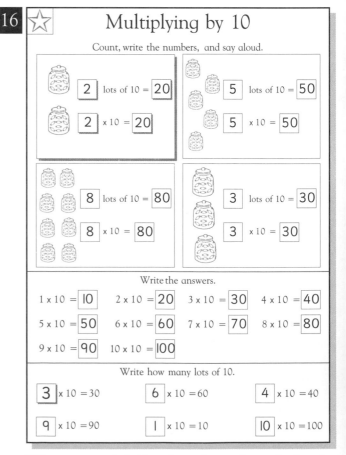

2 lots of 10 = **20**
2 x 10 = **20**

5 lots of 10 = **50**
5 x 10 = **50**

8 lots of 10 = **80**
8 x 10 = **80**

3 lots of 10 = **30**
3 x 10 = **30**

Write the answers.

1 x 10 = **10**   2 x 10 = **20**   3 x 10 = **30**   4 x 10 = **40**

5 x 10 = **50**   6 x 10 = **60**   7 x 10 = **70**   8 x 10 = **80**

9 x 10 = **90**   10 x 10 = **100**

Write how many lots of 10.

3 x 10 = 30   **6** x 10 = 60   **4** x 10 = 40

9 x 10 = 90   **1** x 10 = 10   **10** x 10 = 100

Whatever word children have learnt for multiplication, they should realise that it means 'lots of'. Reinforce the idea that multiplying by a number is really adding that many lots of the number together. 4×10 is the same as 4 lots of 10, and 10+10+10+10.

Multiplying by 5

How many?

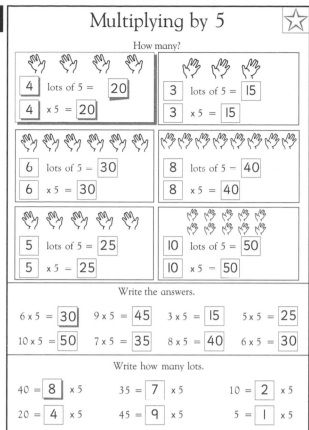

4 lots of 5 = 20
4 x 5 = 20

3 lots of 5 = 15
3 x 5 = 15

6 lots of 5 = 30
6 x 5 = 30

8 lots of 5 = 40
8 x 5 = 40

5 lots of 5 = 25
5 x 5 = 25

10 lots of 5 = 50
10 x 5 = 50

Write the answers.

6 x 5 = 30   9 x 5 = 45   3 x 5 = 15   5 x 5 = 25

10 x 5 = 50   7 x 5 = 35   8 x 5 = 40   6 x 5 = 30

Write how many lots.

40 = 8 x 5   35 = 7 x 5   10 = 2 x 5

20 = 4 x 5   45 = 9 x 5   5 = 1 x 5

Children should remember that the answers in the 5× table always end in 0 or 5. They can use this fact to check their own work to make sure that they do not include any answers that do not fit this rule. Can they also use this to write out the 5× table?

Money

You have only 3 coins in each purse. Draw the 3 coins which make the exact amount needed. You may use each coin more than once.

Limiting the number of coins makes children think more carefully about those they choose to use. It will be helpful to discuss this. They may need help to realise that it is sensible to look for the largest coin to be included first, rather than beginning with the units.

Adding money

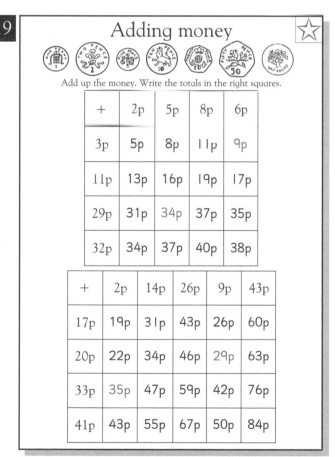

Add up the money. Write the totals in the right squares.

+	2p	5p	8p	6p
3p	5p	8p	11p	9p
11p	13p	16p	19p	17p
29p	31p	34p	37p	35p
32p	34p	37p	40p	38p

+	2p	14p	26p	9p	43p
17p	19p	31p	43p	26p	60p
20p	22p	34p	46p	29p	63p
33p	35p	47p	59p	42p	76p
41p	43p	55p	67p	50p	84p

Remind children that it is money they are adding here, therefore, they must write a 'p' for pence after each answer. Can they talk to you about any short-cuts they have noticed? For instance, when adding 9p, they could add 10p and then take 1p away.

Using doubles

Use the doubles to answer these sums.

6 + 6 = 12	10 + 10 = 20
6 + 7 6 + 6 + 1 = 13	10 + 11 10 + 10 + 1 = 21
6 + 5 6 + 6 − 1 = 11	10 + 9 10 + 10 − 1 = 19

Use doubles to answer these sums.

4 + 4 = 8   4 + 5 = 4 + 4 + 1 = 9

4 + 3 = 4 + 4 − 1 = 7

7 + 7 = 14   7 + 8 = 7 + 7 + 1 = 15

7 + 6 = 7 + 7 − 1 = 13

8 + 8 = 16   9 + 9 = 8 + 9 + 1 = 18

7 + 7 = 8 + 7 − 1 = 14

Double your doubles.

2 double it 4   double it 8   9 double it 18   double it 36

10 double it 20   double it 40   11 double it 22   double it 44

14 double it 28   double it 56   7 double it 14   double it 28

Recognising that a calculation involves two numbers that are almost the same is a useful skill. Doubling the number, and adding or subtracting the 'extra' bit, makes calculation far easier than counting with the whole numbers.

Adding up

Add up the numbers on the sails. Write the totals on the boats.

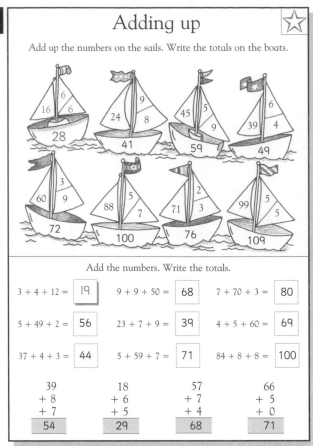

Add the numbers. Write the totals.

3 + 4 + 12 = **19**	9 + 9 + 50 = **68**	7 + 70 + 3 = **80**
5 + 49 + 2 = **56**	23 + 7 + 9 = **39**	4 + 5 + 60 = **69**
37 + 4 + 3 = **44**	5 + 59 + 7 = **71**	84 + 8 + 8 = **100**

39	18	57	66
+ 8	+ 6	+ 7	+ 5
+ 7	+ 5	+ 4	+ 0
54	**29**	**68**	**71**

Help children spot ways to make the calculations easier, e.g. 24+9+8 is easier if they do 24+10+8 and then take one away. For the last boat they may need help to think in terms of 5+5 being added to 100, and the extra 1 being taken away from 110.

Subtraction tables

Finish each table.

−	2	3	5	10
11	9	8	6	1
15	13	12	10	5
20	18	17	15	10

−	1	6	8	9
14	13	8	6	5
19	18	13	11	10
25	24	19	17	16

−	20	14	27	31
52	32	38	25	21
48	28	34	21	17
70	50	56	43	39

Start by asking children to point out on the table where the information is, and where the answer goes. If they find this difficult, try 'sliding' pencils along, one from each of the numbers being used, and letting them meet in the space where the answer should go.

Counting down

The rocket can only lift off at zero.
Use take aways to get back to 0 in 4 moves.

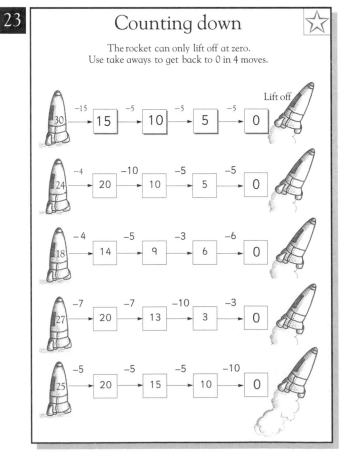

There are many possible answers. If children reach zero too soon, can they split one of their own numbers into two smaller ones and take each away separately? If they can't reach zero, can they add the number they have left to an earlier one and take all of it away in one go?

Clocks

Write the times under the clocks.

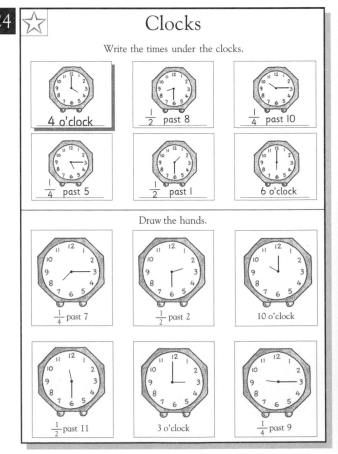

The length of the clock hands is important to ensure that times such as half past 12 and 6 o'clock are not confused. Talk about the shape made from 12 o'clock to $\frac{1}{4}$ past or $\frac{1}{2}$ past. Can they relate this to $\frac{1}{4}$ or $\frac{1}{2}$ of a circle?

Clocks and watches

Write the times.

¼ past 4

½ past 10

9 o' clock

¼ past 5

¼ to 11

¼ to 3

½ past 1

¼ past 11

½ past 7

¼ to 11

¼ to 4

Can children relate any of the times on the clocks to events in their own day? What do they do at $\frac{1}{4}$ to 4 or at 9 o'clock? Help them realise the need for the use of a.m. or p.m. in some cases, so that we can be certain if a time is in the morning, afternoon, or night.

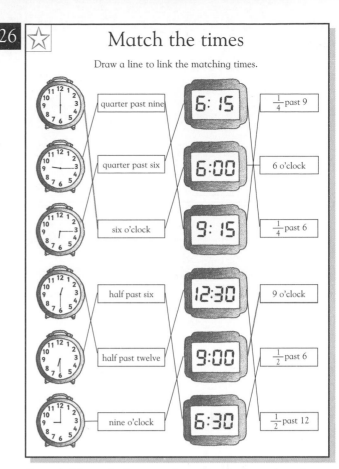

Match the times

Draw a line to link the matching times.

quarter past nine

quarter past six

six o'clock

half past six

half past twelve

nine o'clock

6:15

6:00

9:15

12:30

9:00

6:30

¼ past 9

6 o'clock

¼ past 6

9 o'clock

½ past 6

½ past 12

Can children find examples of both digital and analogue times around the home, such as the video or television? Can they draw both types of clock to show the time they finish school? Talk about other ways of measuring time such as sand-timers or sundials.

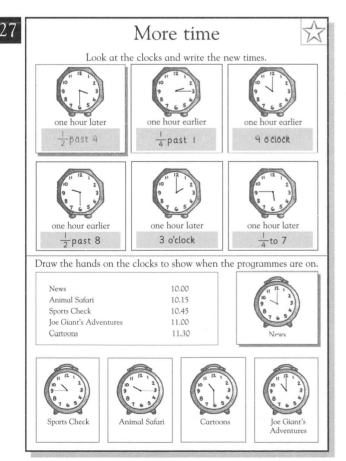

More time

Look at the clocks and write the new times.

one hour later
½ past 4

one hour earlier
¼ past 1

one hour earlier
9 o'clock

one hour earlier
½ past 8

one hour later
3 o'clock

one hour later
¼ to 7

Draw the hands on the clocks to show when the programmes are on.

News	10.00
Animal Safari	10.15
Sports Check	10.45
Joe Giant's Adventures	11.00
Cartoons	11.30

News

Sports Check

Animal Safari

Cartoons

Joe Giant's Adventures

It would be wise to check that the meanings of both 'earlier' and 'later' are fully understood. As an extension, can children draw the clocks, both analogue and digital, to show the times of their own favourite television programmes?

Do you know?

Put the months in order by writing a number on each page.

September 9th
April 4th
February 2nd
August 8th
May 5th
March 3rd
December 12th
June 6th
November 11th
January 1st
October 10th
July 7th

How many...

... seconds in a minute?	60	... minutes in an hour?	60
... hours in a day?	24	... days in a week?	7
... days in a year?	365	... months in a year?	12

Learn this rhyme.

30 days have September,
April, June, and November.
All the rest have 31,
Except February alone
That has 28 days clear
29 in each leap year.

How many days are there in your birthday month?

These numbers are all facts that have to be learned rather than 'found out'. Children can learn the rhyme and then have fun answering questions about the number of days in 'the month Christmas is in' or 'the month we start a new school year'.

Venn diagrams

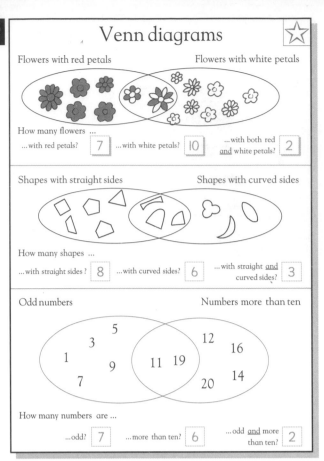

Flowers with red petals · Flowers with white petals

How many flowers ...

...with red petals? **7** ...with white petals? **10** ...with both red and white petals? **2**

Shapes with straight sides · Shapes with curved sides

How many shapes ...

...with straight sides? **8** ...with curved sides? **6** ...with straight and curved sides? **3**

Odd numbers · Numbers more than ten

5
3
1   11 19   12   16
9
7   20   14

How many numbers are ...

...odd? **7** ...more than ten? **6** ...odd and more than ten? **2**

Can children explain why some of the pictures or numbers are in the overlapping part of the two circles? They must remember that these numbers should be included while counting either of the main sets. Draw other flowers or shapes and ask where to include them.

Carroll diagrams

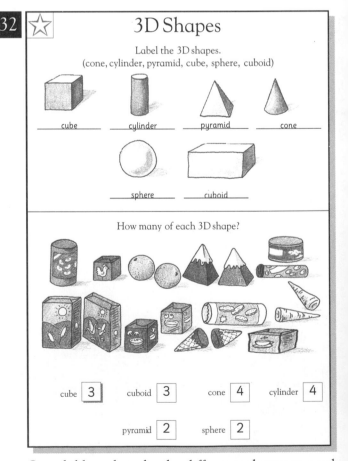

	legs	no legs
green		
not green		

How many creatures are...

... green with no legs **2**

... not green **7**

... not green with legs **3**

... not green with no legs **4**

	Shapes that have 4 sides	Shapes that do not have 4 sides
white		
green		

How many shapes are...

... white **9**

... green with 4 sides **5**

...white but do not have 4 sides **6**

... green but do not have 4 sides **6**

	less than 6	more than 6
odd	1 3 5	7 9 11
even	2 4	8 10 12

How many numbers are...

... odd **6**

... odd and more than 6 **3**

... even and more than 6 **3**

... less than 6 **5**

The most frequently made errors with these diagrams occur when children do not look right down a column or right across a row when counting. Discuss with children issues like where all creatures with legs are drawn and why they are not all in the same box.

2D shapes

Write the name of the shape. Count the corners and sides.

Name **hexagon**
side →
corner → Sides **6** Corners **6**

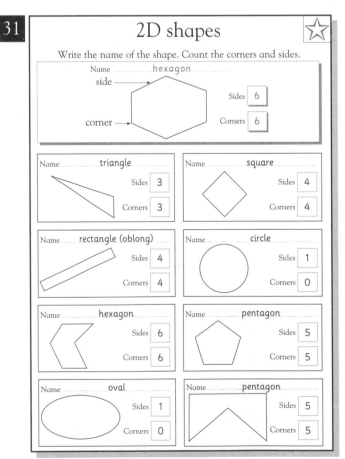

Name **triangle** Sides **3** Corners **3**

Name **square** Sides **4** Corners **4**

Name **rectangle (oblong)** Sides **4** Corners **4**

Name **circle** Sides **1** Corners **0**

Name **hexagon** Sides **6** Corners **6**

Name **pentagon** Sides **5** Corners **5**

Name **oval** Sides **1** Corners **0**

Name **pentagon** Sides **5** Corners **5**

The second figure, though on its end, is still a square and not a diamond. Children may not recognise irregular shapes 5 and 8, but if they count the number of sides they should be able to name them according to that number. For example, any pentagon has 5 sides.

3D Shapes

Label the 3D shapes.
(cone, cylinder, pyramid, cube, sphere, cuboid)

cube   cylinder   pyramid   cone

sphere   cuboid

How many of each 3D shape?

cube **3** cuboid **3** cone **4** cylinder **4**

pyramid **2** sphere **2**

Can children describe the differences between a cube and a cuboid, or a cone and a cylinder? They should be beginning to use appropriate mathematical language such as curved, straight, corners, sides etc.